Cesare Beccaria

250 years

On Crimes and Punishments

Dirk Verhofstadt

The Nine Principles of Cesare Beccaria

Two hundred and fifty years ago, in 1764, Italian philosopher and legal scholar Cesare Beccaria wrote the treatise *Dei delitti e delle pene (On crimes and punishments)*. This book has had a huge impact on our criminal law. Beccaria has substantially contributed to the humanization of criminal law by ridding it of arbitrariness, abuse of power, and religious dogmas. He set a movement in motion that led to the abolition of torture and the death penalty in many countries. This led him to be one of the most influential representatives of the Enlightenment. However, many of his views were not new. He drew inspiration from English philosopher John Locke, French philosophers Charles de Montesquieu, Jean-Jacques Rousseau, and Claude Adrien Helvétius, Scottish philosopher Francis Hutcheson, German legal scholar Christian Thomasius, Austrian lawyer Joseph von Sonnenfels, and Italian thinkers Pietro and Alessandro Verri. Each of them defended a new social order and more humane rules. Beccaria, however, was the first to describe a coherent, logical, rational, and – most importantly – innovative criminal justice system that radically eliminated the foundations of the ancien régime. The then-existing criminal law was repressive, precarious, and barbaric.[1] Punishments were imposed arbitrarily and not everyone was treated equally before the law (insofar as it existed). Perhaps, the best way to summarize the manner of judging and punishing in the ancien

3

régime is by citing the statement of Réal de Curban, a French lawyer and counselor of French King Louis XV: "The sovereign has direct power over the lives and property of his subjects, as well as the punishment for crimes and misdemeanors that disrupt civil society."[2] The arbitrary and horrific criminal justice system of the ancien régime was primarily supported, defended, and applied by religious powers – the Catholic Church in particular.

The work of Cesare Beccaria contains so many innovations in the field of criminal law with regard to legal procedures within the ancien régime that it is difficult to list them all. Therefore, we will limit ourselves to the nine most important. Beccaria's starting point – or rather, his incentive – is already mentioned in his preface. It is the realization of "a maximum level of happiness for a maximum number of people."[3] With this, he joined the utilitarian tradition, which originated in the thinking of Greek philosopher Epicurus and Scottish philosopher David Hume, and which would later be elaborated into a full-fledged system of ethics by English lawyer Jeremy Bentham and philosopher John Stuart Mill. Given that crimes reduce happiness and increase suffering, society should punish them in such a manner that it results in less crimes. Consequently, the purpose of a punishment is not retribution – which adds more suffering to the existing suffering – but preventing that the penalized will cause harm again and deterring others from committing crimes as well.[4] "The purpose of punishment is no different from preventing the offender from harming his fellow

4

citizens again through new criminal offenses and deterring other people from doing the same," Beccaria wrote.[5] In my view, nine fundamental and innovative principles of criminal law are central to *Dei delitti e delle pene*.

In the first place, there is the **principle of legality**, *nulla poena sine lege*. No punishment may be administered without the existence of a law that allows it, and no laws may be created with retroactive effect. "Therefore, the judge who is part of the community has no right to pronounce a sentence that is not recognized by the law on another member of the same society," according to Beccaria.[6] This principle is a means to avoid lawlessness and arbitrariness, but it does maintain several practical conditions. For example, laws should be clear and unequivocal to everyone, which means they should be drafted in a language the people can understand and not merely in Latin, which was usually the case in those days. The author believed that this was required for the sake of justice. "The use of such a foreign language makes the people dependent on a small minority, reduces respect for the legal code – which is intended for openness and for the benefit of everyone – and turns it into an obscure manual, exclusively for the convenience of a few adepts."[7] Beccaria looked at this issue through his utilitarian glasses as well. "The larger the number of citizens that understand the wording of the law and have the legal code in their hands, the less criminality there will be."[8] According to Beccaria, the judge was not allowed to make an interpretation of the law either – a vision that is not always shared in modern criminal law, but that is understandable in the context of the 18th century; as in those days, sentences were pronounced without the existence of a concrete legislative text. With this, the author wanted to prevent judges from pronouncing varying sentences and verdicts that depended on their mood on that particular day for similar violations of the law. He also emphasizes the principle that one is innocent until proven otherwise. "One has no right to consider someone guilty as long as the court has not issued a verdict. (...) If a suspect's guilt is uncertain, one has no right to torture the innocent, because under the law, he who has not been proven guilty of committing the alleged crimes is, indeed, innocent."[9] Lastly, Beccaria advocates for a criminal law that is not focused on vengeance or retribution. "The purpose of punishment cannot be the torment of a sensitive being, nor the striving to undo a crime committed as a result," according to Beccaria, who wanted to make criminal law more rational. French philosopher Michel Foucault also saw the importance of this conversion. "The right to punish has shifted from the sovereign's revenge to the defense of society."[10] This conversion is one of the most important developments in criminal law in human history. It lays the foundation for promoting justice and impeding arbitrariness, and forms the core of a democratic and just society.

In the second place, there is the **principle of equality**. All humans are equal before the law. That means that no one – no nobleman or king either – has more rights than an ordinary citizen. According to

Beccaria, this principle stems from the social contract that each member of society has entered into with the community. Everyone has the same rights and obligations with respect to society. "They (the laws) are binding for anyone, from high to low, both in the royal palace and in the poorest cabin," according to the author.[11] Such a vision was at odds with the practice in the ancien régime that allowed noblemen and clergymen to enjoy all kinds of advantages and privileges. Beccaria disagreed with that. He therefore wrote the following: "Thus, I suggest that criminal sanctions should be the same for the first citizen as well as for the humblest. Any difference in social rank or wealth can only be legitimate if it is based on a pre-established equality before the law, which considers all citizens to be equally subjected to the law."[12] Furthermore, he clarifies that equality prevents the emergence of abuses, which, in turn, is useful for society. "This principle even raises the prestige that laws should enjoy, because it eliminates any opportunity for impunity. If one would argue against me that if the same punishment is imposed on a nobleman and an ordinary citizen, the punishment does, in reality, not mean the same to both as a result from the difference in upbringing and because of the disgrace that is brought upon a notable family. I would like to answer that it is not the sensitivity of the guilty party that indicates the desired proper punishment, but the damage that his crime has caused to society, which is all the greater as the perpetrator was favored by that same society to a greater degree before," Beccaria wrote.[13]

The author was also opposed to the pardon law that was applied by the then-monarch on a regular basis – sometimes out of pity, but more often after the intervention of an influential person. The pardon law breaks the principle of equality and, therefore, the sense of justice. "If one has people believe that forgiveness is possible and that punishment does not necessarily follow the crime, it gives them the illusion that it is possible to escape their righteous punishment. This provides them with the false impression that the execution of sentences for which no pardon was granted is rather an act of the arbitrary abuse of power than a legitimate execution of a decision of the judges. If the monarch grants an amnesty to an offender, does one not rightly claim that he sacrifices the public safety to that of a private person, and that he, in fact, issued a public regulation of impunity through such a special act of misunderstood magnanimity for the benefit of a private person?"[14] In the eyes of Beccaria, the arbitrary granting of pardons to convicts put a brake on a fair judicial process, because punishments do not tolerate exceptions.[15] Finally, he also advocated equality of women in the legal system. He condemned the notion that a woman's testimony would be less valuable than that of a man in an investigation or lawsuit. "Each human being with reason and intelligence – I mean those who are capable of having a certain consistency in their thoughts and who are experiencing the same perceptions as their fellow men – can be accepted as a witness. The true criterion for his credibility is no different than the interest he has in either telling the full truth or not. This sufficiently refutes futile and childish theories which prohibit women from testifying in court because of the weakness of their gender," according to Beccaria.[16]

In the third place, there is the **principle of proportionality**. Punishments should be proportional to the offense committed. This, too, has a utilitarian element, because according to Beccaria, punishments imposed should cause the perpetrator only a minimal level of suffering, yet enough to deter other potential offenders. "Logically, one should give preference to that kind of punishment and that method of implementation which, taking into account their proportion to the offenses committed, leave the people with the most efficient and lasting impression, and which the offender still experiences as the least cruel at firsthand," the author wrote.[17] A logic result from this is, therefore, that the best punishment is a punishment that is both moderate and effective. This vision also caused commotion, and it conflicted with practices common in those days. Small perpetrators of minor offenses were often horribly punished by cutting of a hand or other limbs, whereas noblemen who had committed serious crimes got off the hook with a fine, if they were even punished at all. However, the central focus remained on Beccaria's vision that many punishments of his day were too gruesome and missed their purpose. "The excessive cruelty of the punishment even has the opposite effect, because the offender will take even more risks to avoid his punishment, in proportion as the suffering that threatens him is greater. The result is that various criminal offenses are committed in order to escape the punishment for a single offense," the author wrote.[18]

The fourth element in his *Dei delitti e delle pene* is the **principle of subsidiarity**, which, in fact, arises from the principle of proportionality. According to Beccaria, it is, for example, better to impose a minimal punishment than either no punishment at all or a ruthlessly severe punishment. If one wishes to prevent crime wherever possible, one's inability to escape punishment is more important than a punishment being cruel. "The certainty that one will be punished, albeit without excessive grimness, will definitely leave man with a deeper impression than the risk of another, much heavier sanction, from which one still surreptitiously hopes to be able to escape. The smallest suffering makes man flinch if he sees there is no escaping from it. For greater pain, on the other hand, there is always that heavenly gift of hope – that balm for all wounds – which prevents us from being aware of the threat of great suffering; particularly when the example of impunity, which is so frequently obtained as a result of weakness and bribery, causes this hopeful anticipation to increase in strength."[19] Consequently, only the strictly necessary amount of force and power may be used in the investigation and punishment. It is a clear principle, but its execution is not always that simple. After all, a powerful government tends to deploy means that are too severe, whilst public opinion also believes that the measures taken are too soft. The principle of subsidiarity should curb criminal justice agencies and keep punishments within the limits of reasonableness, no matter how difficult that occasionally may be due to the pressure from public opinion. Criminal justice should be and remain an *ultimum remedium*. That is also the view of criminologist and Professor Brice de Ruyver from Ghent, who states that one should not rely on criminal justice until "other regulatory mechanisms are failing in society and if essential values are involved that must absolutely be protected by criminal law."[20] Moreover, with the principle of subsidiarity, the switch was made from a criminal justice system that is based on retribution to a system that strives towards prevention and reasonableness. "People should fear the laws, but nothing else than the laws," because laws exist for the very reason of protecting the rights and freedom of man.[21]

The fifth is the **principle of abolitionism** in respect of torture and the death penalty. To Beccaria, torture was simply a barbaric practice. According to him, a confession obtained through torture was a useless confession. Particularly modern was the link with the vision that no one has the right to consider someone guilty as long as he or she has not been convicted by a court. Put differently, society should protect the human integrity of suspects from the power of the government as well. Beccaria wrote the following about this: "A law that dictates torture using the rack is a law that says, 'People, resist physical pain.' If nature has provided you with an indestructible self-love and an undeniable right to defense, I force you towards a completely opposite feeling, namely, a feeling of heroic hatred against your own person. I command you to sue yourself and tell the

11

truth, even if your bones had to be broken in doing so. This horrible crucible of the truth is the extant remnant of earlier barbaric legislation that perceived the test of fire or boiling water and the volatile results of the judicial dilemma as a trial by ordeal. It reasoned from the rationale that God is constantly concerned with the people and intervenes in a particular way to settle each of their futile disagreements."[22] This view was diametrically opposed to the belief that God can punish man in this life and encountered a lot of opposition. Beccaria, however, defended his stance using rational arguments. "A peculiar, but unavoidable consequence of torture is that it causes the innocent to be placed in a less favorable position than the guilty suspect. If both are put on the rack, the innocent, in any eventuality, has everything to lose. The innocent will either confess the imputed crime and be wrongfully convicted, or his innocence will be recognized, but he will have suffered the horrors of an undeserved punishment in the meantime. For the guilty, however, there is one chance for a favorable outcome. If he effectually defies torture, he must be allowed to get off scot-free as an innocent man. He, therefore, succeeded in reducing the greater punishment he actually deserved to a smaller one," according to Beccaria.[23]

Even more controversial was his rejection of the death penalty save for two exceptions. First, the death of a few fellow citizens can be necessary in difficult moments "at which a nation is on the verge of losing or recapturing its freedom, or in times of anarchy, when unrest and revolt lay down the law."[24] Second, if death "is the true and only means to prevent others from committing new crimes."[25] These exceptions have a distinctive utilitarian nature, and to Beccaria, they form absolute exceptions to the rule of principle that the death penalty should be abolished. "To which right can people refer themselves in order to murder their fellowmen?"[26] It is a crucial question that continues to be debated. Again, Beccaria cites reasons for refraining from applying such a punishment. "Experience throughout the ages proves that the threat of the death penalty has never succeeded in stopping people from committing misdeeds."[27] According to him, prolonged prison sentences are more humane and form a better deterrent than the death penalty. "It is not the intensity of the punishment, but its duration that exerts the greatest influence on the human mind. (...) The horrific, yet transient spectacle that the execution of a criminal can offer is a less powerful repellent than the lasting and striking example of a human being who is deprived of his freedom and who, lowered to the rank of a beast of burden, has to reimburse society for what he has done to it."[28]

Number six is the **principle of rationality**. Punishments may not be pronounced based on irrational accusations such as heresy, witchcraft, and 'unnatural' acts (homosexuality), as Montesquieu had argued before. This vision was met with a lot of opposition from the Catholic Church, which saw its moral dominance jeopardized, as to the Church, heresy, witchcraft, and unnatural acts remained the subjects of the Inquisition's investigation and prosecution that

13

usually ended with the burning of the perpetrator on the stake. The author turned squarely against these practices and wrote somewhat cynically: "The preachers of the Gospel truth dared to propagate the God of love and mercy with their blood-soaked hands every day."[29] A little further, he added: "In the case of sorcery, it is more likely that the witnesses are lying."[30] Beccaria thought it was equally irrational to punish suicides, which still often occurred in the ancien régime in the form of a posthumous punishment. For example, the corpse was frequently dishonored by dragging it through town behind a horse and cart and by burying it in unconsecrated ground. Even worse was the confiscation of the possessions and properties of the person who committed suicide at the expense of close relatives. Beccaria opposed this. "Whoever is deterred by the suffering of the punishment, shall abide by the laws. However, we should not forget that death puts an end to all physical suffering. What rational and convincing reasoning, then, is strong enough to prevent the hand of the person committing suicide from carrying out his act of desperation? (...) It is futile to enact laws which constitute no sanctions or which are made unenforceable by circumstances."[31] From the same rational and utilitarian approach, Beccaria also advocates practical measures which can cause the number of crimes to decrease: "The streets should be illuminated at night at the expense of the community, and sufficient police force should be divided across the various districts of the cities."[32]

The seventh element in his *Dei delitti e delle pene* is the **principle of personality**, meaning "only the criminal may be punished, and no innocent third parties."[33] The criminal law in those days required that the criminals as well as their family members were punished. In many instances, this involved the confiscation of the properties of the perpetrator, causing the wife and children to lose all their possessions and fall into complete poverty. Especially in the case of the death penalty and banishment, all the goods that belonged to him (or her) and the entire family were declared forfeited. Beccaria opposed this using strong terms: "The application of the declaration of forfeiture constantly puts a price on the heads of those who are the most defenseless, and it subjects the innocent to punishments that are intended for criminals. Moreover, it induces plenty of honorable people to resort to crime in order to save themselves from their desperate situation. Is there a more horrible spectacle than the image of an entire family that is thrown into misery and sees its good name being dragged through the mud because of the crimes of the head of the family? Especially when the existing institution of paternal authority would not even legally permit family members to oppose the head of the family, even if this would be possible in material terms."[34] The use of the general declaration of forfeiture was prohibited by most Western constitutions later on. However, the special declaration of confiscation still exists, which, for example, applies to goods or materials that are the object of the crime or served it, as well as to the material benefits that resulted from the crime, such as money or a stolen object. Beccaria had already anticipated that, too: "Therefore, in relation to the severity of the crime committed, instances must exist to which an overall confiscation of goods is applied, and others, which provide a partial confiscation, and still other instances, in which a confiscation is not possible at all."[35] However, the principle of personality also has to do with another aspect of criminal law, namely, the application of the criminal law to subjects who are guilty of committing a crime in another country.

The eighth principle defended by Beccaria is the **principle of laicization**. He does not oppose the existence of God or the divine right that was generally accepted in those days – even if it was just to avoid evoking the wrath of the Inquisition (Beccaria was clearly afraid of being regarded as an atheist). However, it is already in his preface that he makes clear that a specific "human right" exists as well. "The divine law and the natural law are immutable and constant through their essence, because the relationship between two similar things will always remain the same. However, as the human right, or, in other words, the right of a particular state or community, merely constitutes the relationship between a certain action and a changeable social situation, in which society finds itself at that particular moment, this human right can also differ, depending on whether that action shall be necessary or useful for the community."[36] Similarly, Beccaria also rejects a 'trial by ordeal' and punishment based on magic. It is not up to theologians to decide what is beneficial or harmful for society; it is up to judges who follow the law written by people. This comes down to a laicization of the public order. It entails a breach with the then-common practices, which involved infringements on religious grounds, such as blasphemy, sacrilege, and other offenses of ecclesiastical provisions, and which led to nearly one fourth to one third of all punishments.[37] The mid-eighteenth-century executions of Jean Calas and François-Jean Lefebvre de La Barre constitute some telling examples of this. Lastly, Beccaria turned against the so-called right of asylum, which allowed fugitives to hide in churches and other 'sacred' places where they were unreachable for the secular power, which severely impeded the fight against crime. "Within the borders of a country, there must be no place that is placed above the law. The strong arm of the law should be able to follow each citizen, as the shadow follows the human body," according to Beccaria.[38] The Catholic Church, which held on to the privilege of the right of asylum, was not appreciative of that either.

The ninth principle is the **principle of publicity**. Beccaria argued for public trials and advocated against any form of a secret procedure and anonymous allegations. Beccaria literally writes that the principle of legality requires that laws are clear and comprehensible to everyone.[39] Consequently, secret laws are unacceptable to the author. Hearings, rulings, and punishments should have a public nature as well. This, too, contains a utilitarian element. "The intention of this regulation (public hearings) is to allow public opinion, which is perhaps the only cement in society, to exert an inhibiting effect on violence and passions, so that the people may say: 'We are not slaves, we are protected by the law.'"[40] With this, Beccaria joined the vision of Baruch Spinoza. "Whoever is able to handle state affairs in secrecy has the state in his power unconditionally and is as great a threat to citizens in peacetime as to the enemy in wartime."[41] In a similar vein, he follows Montesquieu on the necessity of the public nature of allegations.[42] "An obvious, but deep-rooted ailment, which is even necessary in many countries because of the weakness of the state system, are secret accusations. These turn people into liars and tricksters. He who can suspect his neighbor of being a snitch, will soon see an enemy in him," Beccaria wrote.[43] Secret indictments and secret processes were objectionable in his eyes. These were practices that were considered normal in many countries. "If I had to implement new laws in some deserted corner of the world, my hands would be shaking, and I would rethink it ten times before I would allow the system of secret accusations there; and I would recognize its disastrous consequences for the future in hundredfold."[44] The great extent to which Beccaria cared about the public nature of processes and the administering of appropriate punishments is also evident from the conclusion of his book. "To avoid that whatever punishment would be an act of violence of a single person or of many against one citizen in particular, they should be truly public, be pronounced as soon as possible, be necessary, and, under the given circumstances, they should be the least severe, in the right proportion to the crime committed, and required by the law."[45]

At the end of his book, Beccaria refers to the importance of a good upbringing as the best tool in the fight against crime. "Finally, the most reliable – but also the most difficult – way to prevent crime is to improve the upbringing."[46] To Beccaria, a better upbringing formed the key to more ethical – or let us call it less violent – behavior. This view was later defended by other Enlightenment thinkers as well. It encouraged the organization of public education for all children. Beccaria was not the first to do so, but he was an important advocate of education and upbringing, which should result in a more humane and peaceful society.

The views of Beccaria remain topical because there are still countries where people are being tortured and executed, where alleged criminals do not get a lawyer, where hearings take place in secret, where heresy and blasphemy are being punished, where people are arbitrarily punished while there is no law that allows it, where people are being punished for minor offenses in an unreasonably severe manner, where people are being prosecuted and arrested without a court order, where no independent judiciary exists, where homosexuals get the death penalty, where suicide is being punished, and where the *lex talionis* is still being applied. All these practices run counter to the principles of *Dei delitti e delle pene*, to the Universal as well as the European Declaration of Human Rights, and to the liberal fundamental principles that form the basis of a true democratic constitutional state. Although different in intensity and weightiness, these practices are found in almost all countries of the world – in our regions as well. Though whoever thinks that Western democracies, for example, do not commit violations of the basic principles of the constitutional state, is straying from the truth. In fact, over the past decades, there is a tendency among governments to use excessive power when dealing with citizens, who, as a result, are once again subject to a certain degree of arbitrariness. For that very reason, it is so important to reread, study, and apply the ideas that Beccaria wrote down 250 years ago. In that sense, *Dei delitti e delle pene* is a highly topical book that should be shown to all those political, military, religious and other leaders who are violating human rights and who are trampling upon freedom and justice, and we should confront them with it.

Dirk Verhofstadt
Professor 'Media and Ethics' University of Ghent

Bibliografy

Audegean Philippe (2010), *La philosophe de Beccaria. Savoir punir, savoir écrire, savoir produire*, VRIN

Balthazar, T., Christiaens, J., Cools, M., Decorte, T., De Ruyver, B., Hebberecht, P., Ponsaers, P., Snacken, S., Traest, P., Vander Beken, T. en Vermeulen, G. (eds.), *Update in de criminologie, Het strafrechtssysteem in de Laatmoderniteit* (2004), Universiteit Gent, Mechelen, Kluwer

Beccaria Cesare (1971), *Over misdaden en straffen*, Foreword from J.M. van Bemmelen, Standaard Uitgeverij

Beccaria Cesare (1982), *Over misdaden en straffen*, Foreword from J.M. van Bemmelen Kluwer Rechtswetenschappen

Bellamy Richard (1995), *Beccaria: 'On Crimes and Punishments' and Other Writings*, Cambridge University Press

Bentham Jeremy (1823), *An Introduction to the Principles of Morals and Legislation*, Oxford, Clarendon Press

Foucault Michel (1989), *Discipline, Toezicht en Straf*, Historische Uitgeverij

Hostettler John (2010), *Cesare Beccaria. The Genius of 'On Crimes and Punishments'*, Waterside Press

Maestro Marcello (1973), *Cesare Beccaria and the Origins of Penal Reform*, Temple University Press

Monbally Jos (2010), *Zes eeuwen strafrecht. De geschiedenis van het Belgische strafrecht*, Acco

Montesquieu (2006), *Over de geest van de wetten*, Boom

Porret Michel (1997), *Beccaria et la Culture Juridique des Lumières*, Librairie Droz

Spinoza B. de (2014), *Staatkundige Verhandeling* (1677), Wereldbibliotheek Amsterdam

Van Dijk Alwin Auke (2008), *Strafrechterlijke aansprakelijkheid heroverwogen: over opzet, schuld, schulduitsluitingsgronden en straf,* Maklu-Uitgevers

Voltaire (2013), *Traité sur la Tolérance, A l'occasion de la mort de Jean Calas*, Librio Philosophie

Voltaire (2013), *Relation de la mort du chevalier de La Barre, par Monsieur Cass**** , Hachette Livre,

Witteveen Willem (1996), *De geordende wereld van het recht: een inleiding*, Amsterdam University Press

Endnotes

[1] E. Monachesi, *Pioneers in Criminology. IX Cesare Beccharia (1738-1794)*, Journal of Criminal Law and Criminology, Volume 46, 1956, p. 441.

[2] G. de Réal de Curban, *La science du gouvernement, ouvrage de morale, de droit et de politique*, Tome Quatrieme, 1765, p. 445. Quoted in: Michel Porret, *Beccaria et la Culture Juridique des Lumières*, Librairie Droz, 1997, p. 11.

[3] C. Beccaria, *Over misdaden en straffen*, Kluwer rechtswetenschappen, 1982, p. 37.

[4] A. Auke van Dijk, *Strafrechterlijke aansprakelijkheid heroverwogen: over opzet, schuld,schuldduitsluitingsgronden en straf*, Maklu-Uitgevers, 2008, p. 88.

[5] C. Beccaria, *Over misdaden en straffen*, Kluwer rechtswetenschappen, 1982, p. 101.

[6] Idem, p. 45.

[7] Idem, p. 55.

[8] Idem, p. 55.

[9] C. Beccaria, *Over misdaden en straffen*, Kluwer rechtswetenschappen, 1982, p. 79-80.

[10] M. Foucault, *Discipline, Toezicht en Straf*, Historische Uitgeverij, 1989, p. 126.

[11] C. Beccaria, *Over misdaden en straffen*, Kluwer rechtswetenschappen, 1982, p. 49.

[12] Idem, p. 157.

[13] Idem, p. 157-158.

[14] Idem, p. 134.

[15] P. Audegean, *La philosophe de Beccaria. Savoir punir, savoir écrire, savoir produire*, VRIN, 2010, p. 67.

[16] C. Beccaria, *Over misdaden en straffen*, Kluwer rechtswetenschappen, 1982, p. 67.

[17] Idem, p. 101-102.

[18] Idem, p. 104.

[19] Idem, p. 132.

[20] B. De Ruyver, *Het strafrechtelijk beleid in een postmoderne samenleving*, Balthazar, T., Christiaens, J., Cools, M., Decorte, T., De Ruyver, B., Hebberecht, P., Ponsaers, P., Snacken, S., Traest, P., Vander Beken, T. en Vermeulen, G. (eds.), *Update in de criminologie, Het strafrechtssysteem in de Laatmoderniteit*, Universiteit Gent, Mechelen, Kluwer, 2004, p. 155-156.

[21] W. Witteveen, *De geordende wereld van het recht: een inleiding*, Amsterdam University Press, 1996, p. 321.

[22] C. Beccaria, *Over misdaden en straffen*, Kluwer rechtswetenschappen, 1982, p. 81.

[23] Idem, p. 84.

[24] Idem, p. 109.

[25] Idem, p. 109.

[26] Idem, p. 107.

[27] Idem, p. 109.

[28] Idem, p. 110.

[29] Idem, p. 57.

[30] Idem, p. 70.

[31] Idem, p. 179-180.

[32] Idem, p. 174.

[33] J. Monbally, *Zes eeuwen strafrecht. De geschiedenis van het Belgische strafrecht (1400-2000)*, Acco, 2010, p. 41.

[34] C. Beccaria, *Over misdaden en straffen*, Kluwer rechtswetenschappen, 1982, p.

124.

[35] Idem, p. 123.

[36] Idem, p. 33.

[37] M. Porret, *Beccaria et la Culture Juridique des Lumières*, Librairie Droz, 1997, p. 110-111.

[38] C. Beccaria, *Over misdaden en straffen*, Kluwer rechtswetenschappen, 1982, p. 136.

[39] W. Witteveen, *De geordende wereld van het recht: een inleiding*, Amsterdam University Press, 1996, p. 321.

[40] C. Beccaria, *Over misdaden en straffen*, Kluwer rechtswetenschappen, 1982, p. 66.

[41] B. de Spinoza, *Staatkundige Verhandeling*, uit het Latijn vertaald en toegelicht door Karel D'Huyvetters, Introduced by Jonathan Israel, Wereldbibliotheek Amsterdam, 2014, p. 161.

[42] Montesquieu, *Over de geest van de wetten*, Boom, 2006, p. 278.

[43] C. Beccaria, *Over misdaden en straffen*, Kluwer rechtswetenschappen, 1982, p. 72.

[44] Idem, p. 74.

[45] Idem, p. 46.

[46] Idem, p. 214.

www.ingramcontent.com/pod-product-compliance
Lightning Source LLC
Chambersburg PA
CBHW021001180526
45163CB00006B/2458